MW01124528

GIRL CODE REVOLUTION

PROFILES AND PROJECTS TO INSPIRE CODERS

SHEELA PREUITT

Lerner Publications ◆ Minneapolis

DEDICATED TO SHRADDHA AND SABURI

Children should always ask permission before going online, especially when using a new website. Stay safe online by protecting your identity. Never share personal information such as your full name, address, or email address online. Think carefully about posting personal photos of yourself, your friends, and your family.

Lerner Publications Company
An imprint of Lerner Publishing Group, Inc.
241 First Avenue North
Minneapolis, MN 55401 USA

For reading levels and more information, look up this title at www.lernerbooks.com.

Main body text set in Aptifer Sans LT Pro.
Typeface provided by Linotype AG.

Editor: Allison Juda **Designer**: Lindsey Owens

Library of Congress Cataloging-in-Publication Data

Names: Preuitt, Sheela, author.
Title: Girl code revolution : profiles and projects to inspire coders / Sheela Preuitt.
Description: Minneapolis : Lerner Publications, 2021. | Includes bibliographical references and index.
 | Audience: Ages 8–12 | Audience: Grades 4–6 | Summary: "Part how-to, part profile, and all about
 getting girls coding. Step-by-step instructions for projects girls actually want to code and profiles
 of aspirational female coders in the field combine to lead the girl code revolution" —Provided by
 publisher.
Identifiers: LCCN 2019052537 (print) | LCCN 2019052538 (ebook) | ISBN 9781541596726 (lib. bdg.)
 | ISBN 9781728400648 (eb pdf)
Subjects: LCSH: Computer programming—Juvenile literature.
Classification: LCC QA76.6115 .P74 2021 (print) | LCC QA76.6115 (ebook) | DDC 005.13078—dc23

LC record available at https://lccn.loc.gov/2019052537
LC ebook record available at https://lccn.loc.gov/2019052538

Manufactured in the United States of America
2-50182-48217-1/26/2021

CONTENTS

WOMEN CODERS

WOMEN HAVE ALWAYS BEEN AT THE FOREFRONT OF SOFTWARE DEVELOPMENT, THOUGH THEY HAVE NOT ALWAYS RECEIVED THE RECOGNITION THEY DESERVE. In the nineteenth century, Ada Lovelace predicted the power of computers. Margaret Hamilton helped develop software that took us to the moon. And websites like Pinterest and Quora would be very different without the input of Tracy Chou.

These women contributed to the field of computer science and software engineering using their passion and perseverance. They loved what they did, and they did it well, disproving stereotypes that women were not suited for careers in STEM.

Coding can be a fun and powerful way to get your message across. Gather some friends, and use your imagination to get coding!

Build and test your coding skills by following along with the online instructions at the Vidcode Lerner sandbox. Create an account that will allow you to save and customize your personal projects.

PAGE PLUS

FOLLOW ALONG WITH YOUR OWN CODING AT QRS.LERNERBOOKS.COM /GIRLCODE.

vidcode

DOGE MEME

PROJECT TIME:
10 MINUTES

CODING CONCEPTS:
VARIABLES, OBJECTS,
PROPERTIES

Add text to an image or video clip to create a meme using the programming language JavaScript. Objects and their properties make creating memes easy with just a few lines of code.

1. Click on the text block in the Effects tab. The code in the code editor represents a variable. The variable's name is my_text1, and it holds your text object.

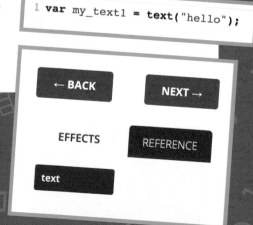

```
1 var my_text1 = text("hello");
```

← BACK   NEXT →

EFFECTS   REFERENCE

text

2. You can change text properties such as size, color, and message by adding lines of code below the text object. Each line of code should be on its own line and end with a semicolon.

```
1 var my_text1 = text("hello");
2 my_text1.message = "much variable";
3 my_text1.color = "yellow";
4 my_text1.size = 40;
```

3. From the Graphics tab, select a doge image. This is your graphic object.

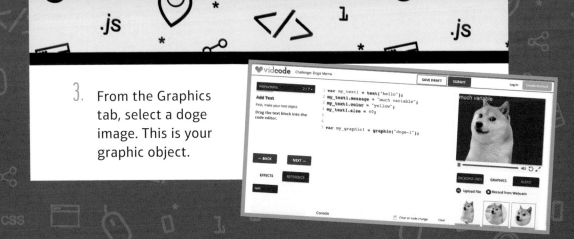

4. You can change properties such as x-position (left and right), y-position (up and down), and size of the graphic object by adding lines of code.

```
6
7 var my_graphic1 = graphic("doge-1");
8 my_graphic1.x = 20;
9 my_graphic1.y = 100;
10 my_graphic1.scale = 0.5;
```

ADA LOVELACE

1815–1852

MATHEMATICIAN AND COMPUTER VISIONARY

ADA LOVELACE PLAYED A BIG ROLE IN COMPUTER PROGRAMMING. As a teenager, Ada met mathematics professor Charles Babbage. In 1843 she translated an article from French to English about Babbage's Analytical Engine, an early computer design. Lovelace added notes in her translation that were much longer than the original article.

She described how the Analytical Engine could use step-by-step instructions to perform tasks. Because of this, many consider Lovelace to be the first computer programmer.

"MATHEMATICAL SCIENCE SHOWS WHAT IS. . . . BUT TO USE AND APPLY THAT LANGUAGE, WE MUST BE ABLE FULLY TO APPRECIATE, TO FEEL, TO SEIZE THE UNSEEN."

—ADA LOVELACE

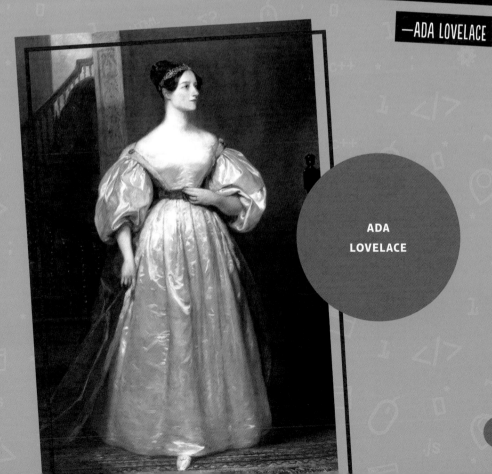

ADA LOVELACE

DOODLE AUGMENTED REALITY

PROJECT TIME: 15 MINUTES

CODING CONCEPTS:
OBJECTS AND PROPERTIES

With just a few lines of code, you can create a one-of-a-kind doodle to enhance your video.

1. Click on a video from the Backgrounds tab.

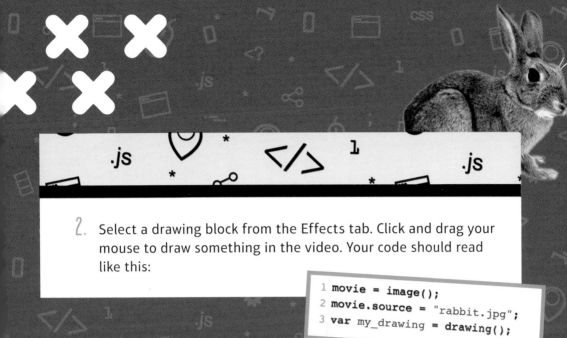

2. Select a drawing block from the Effects tab. Click and drag your mouse to draw something in the video. Your code should read like this:

```
1 movie = image();
2 movie.source = "rabbit.jpg";
3 var my_drawing = drawing();
```

3. Change the properties of your drawing by adding lines of code in your code editor such as these:

```
3 var my_drawing = drawing();
4 my_drawing.color = "orange";
5 my_drawing.lineWidth = 4;
6 my_drawing.x = 80;
7 my_drawing.y = -70;
8 my_drawing.rotation = -25;
```

GRACE HOPPER

1906–1992

COMPUTER LANGUAGE CREATOR

AFTER EARNING A PHD IN MATHEMATICS FROM YALE UNIVERSITY IN 1934, a rare accomplishment for a woman at the time, Grace Hopper worked with early computer technology. Noticing that repetitive calculations done by hand were prone to errors, she created code to replace the manual work. Hopper was also the first to coin the terms *computer bug* and *debugging* after discovering that a moth stuck to one of the switches of a computer had caused it to glitch.

Hopper is known as the mother of COBOL, an early programming language that led to many other coding languages. Hopper believed that anyone should be able to program. Her life's work made it so that you can too!

"TO ME PROGRAMMING IS MORE THAN AN IMPORTANT PRACTICAL ART. IT IS ALSO A GIGANTIC UNDERTAKING IN THE FOUNDATIONS OF KNOWLEDGE."

—GRACE HOPPER

GRACE HOPPER

SURPRISE EMOJI

Get ready to create a random emoji generator using the Math object!

.js </> .js

1. Select a video from the Backgrounds tab.

2. An array stores a list of items in one variable. Create a variable called "my_emojis" to hold an empty array.

```
1 movie = video();
2 movie.source = "monarch-butterfly.mp4";
3 var my_emojis = [];
```

.js </> .js

3. Fill the array with some emojis.

4. Select a text block. Replace "hello" with the first emoji in your "my_emojis" array. Programmers start counting from zero, so the first emoji in the array is item zero.

```
3 var my_emojis = ["🐛","🐞","😀","😂"];
4 var my_text1 = text(my_emojis[0]);
```

14

5. Try changing the number inside your bracket from my_emojis[0] to my_emojis[1]. What happens in the video?

6. Figure out the length, or number of items, in your array. Add a variable called "len" above the line of text code, and make it equal to the length of your emojis array.

```
3 var my_emojis = ["😈","😇","😂","😅"];
4 var len = my_emojis.length;
5 var my_text1 = text(my_emojis[1]);
```

7. Add the line of code var random_number = Math.random(); above your text code. This will generate a number between 0 and 1 and store it in the variable called "random_number." Multiply this by the length of the "my_emojis" array.

8. Round the "random_number" down to a whole number using "floor."

9. Change the number inside your text code to "random_number."

```
1 movie = video();
2 movie.source = "monarch-butterfly.mp4";
3 var my_emojis = ["😈","😇","😂","😅"];
4 var len = my_emojis.length;
5 var random_number = Math.floor(Math.random() * len);
6 var my_text1 = text(my_emojis[random_number]);
```

10. Restart your video. A random emoji from your array should appear.

ANNIE EASLEY

1933–2011

COMPUTER PROGRAMMER, ROCKET SCIENTIST, AND EQUAL EMPLOYMENT ADVOCATE

ANNIE EASLEY STARTED AT THE NATIONAL ADVISORY COMMITTEE FOR AERONAUTICS, the organization that became NASA, doing calculations by hand. When computers replaced humans, Easley became a skilled programmer. Her code helped analyze power technology, leading to a battery design for the Centaur rocket, as well as for early hybrid cars.

Easley actively worked to make STEM fields more inclusive. She encouraged women and other underrepresented groups to pursue STEM education. She also helped address issues of race, gender, and age discrimination in the workplace.

"IF I CAN'T WORK WITH YOU, I WILL WORK AROUND YOU. . . . I'M SURE, I, LIKE MANY OTHERS, HAVE BEEN JUDGED NOT ON WHAT I CAN DO, BUT ON WHAT I LOOK LIKE. . . . [BUT] I WOULD NOT LET THAT GET ME DOWN."

—ANNIE EASLEY

ANNIE EASLEY

ANIMATE A RAINBOW

PROJECT TIME:
20 MINUTES

CODING CONCEPTS:
LOOPS, ARRAYS,
RANDOM NUMBERS

Learn how to apply tint to your image to change its color.

.js   </>   1   .js

1. Click on a video from the Backgrounds tab to get started. Select the tint effect.

2. Edit the tint code to save it in a variable.

3. Create a list of colors you want to use in an array.

```
4  var my_tint = tint("red", 50);
5  var my_colors =
   ["red","orange","pink","green","blue"];
```

.js   </>   1   .js

4. To find out the number of items in the array, use the "length" property.

```
6  var numColors = my_colors.length;
```

5. Drag a repeat block into the code editor.

```
4  var my_tint = tint("red", 50);
5  var my_colors =
   ["red","orange","pink","green","blue"];
6  var numColors = my_colors.length;
7  repeat(function() {
8      //write code below
9
10 }, 5);
```

6. Inside the repeat block code, create a variable to hold a random number and a variable to get a random color from the array. Then set the "my_tint" color property to use this random color value.

```
7  repeat(function() {
8      //write code below
9      var randNum =
   Math.floor(numColors*Math.random());
10     var myColor = my_colors[randNum];
11     my_tint.color = myColor;
12 }, 5);
```

7. Change the last number in the repeat block to cycle through the colors faster or slower.

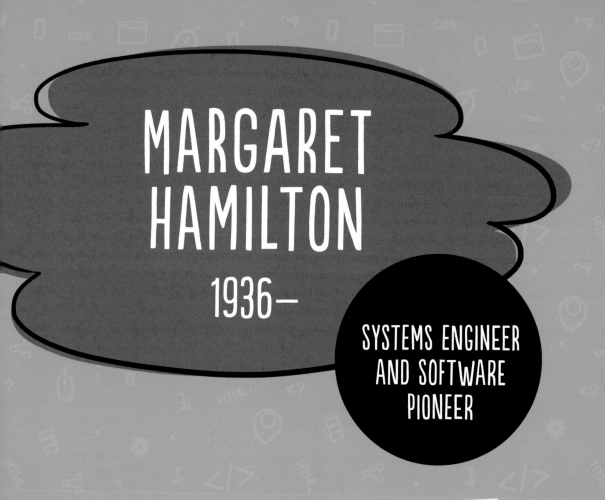

MARGARET HAMILTON

1936–

SYSTEMS ENGINEER AND SOFTWARE PIONEER

MARGARET HAMILTON'S LIFELONG LOVE FOR MATH LED HER TO PROGRAMMING. At Massachusetts Institute of Technology (MIT), Hamilton worked with programs for predicting the weather and identifying aircraft, as well as leading the team that created software for the Apollo space missions. She grew passionate about designing systems that were dependable and efficient, and that could detect errors and recover information after a crash. She is credited with coining the term *software engineer*. She has always had a fearless approach to problem-solving and a belief that all people should have access to education and a career of their choice.

"COMING UP WITH NEW IDEAS WAS AN ADVENTURE. DEDICATION AND COMMITMENT WERE A GIVEN. . . . THERE WAS NO CHOICE BUT TO BE PIONEERS."

—MARGARET HAMILTON

MARGARET HAMILTON

SFX LASERS

PROJECT TIME:
20 MINUTES

CODING CONCEPTS:
CONDITIONALS

Try creating a video that includes shooting lasers.

1. Select a video from the Backgrounds tab and a drawing block from the Effects tab.

2. Draw your laser line. Set the color of your laser using the color property.

```
4 var my_drawing = drawing();
5 my_drawing.color = "orange";
```

3. Hover over the time at the bottom of your video to see "movie.currentTime" display. The current time of your video is stored in this variable.

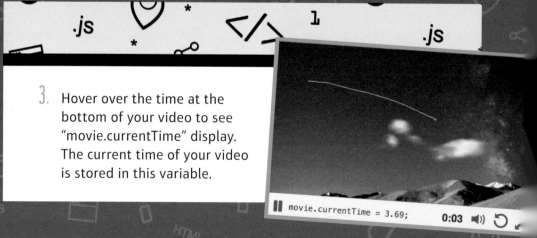

```
movie.currentTime = 3.69;        0:03
```

4. Pause your video when you want to start and stop the laser, and note the values of "movie.currentTime." Create two variables to hold these values.

```
4 var my_drawing = drawing();
5 my_drawing.color = "orange";
6 var laserStart = 2.55;
7 var laserEnd = 4.15;
```

5. From the Effects tab, choose the repeat block. Click inside the code, and select the if-else block from the same tab.

6. Replace what's inside the parentheses with the conditional.

```
9  repeat(function() {
10     //write code below
11
12     //replace true with a conditional statement
   below
13     if(movie.currentTime > laserStart &&
   movie.currentTime < laserEnd) {
14
15     } else {
16
17     }
```

7. Next, set the position of the drawing.

8. Set the else block so the laser will be off-screen before the start value and after the end value. Your conditional if-else code should look like this:

```
12     if(movie.currentTime > laserStart &&
   movie.currentTime < laserEnd) {
13         my_drawing.x = 0;
14     } else {
15         my_drawing.x = 1000;
16     }
17 }, 5);
```

23

TRACY CHOU
1987–

SOFTWARE ENGINEER AND ENTREPRENEUR

TRACY CHOU GREW UP IN SAN FRANCISCO, CALIFORNIA, WITH COMPUTER-SCIENTIST PARENTS.

Chou studied electrical engineering and computer science in school and earned internships at Facebook and Google. She played major roles at Quora and Pinterest when these companies were just concepts.

Chou sought to change the lack of diversity in the technology field. She cofounded Project Include and asked major tech companies to share their diversity data. As an entrepreneur and activist, she combats online harassment and abuse through her start-up, Block Party. The company builds tools that help people remove negative content from social media.

"DON'T GET CAUGHT UP IN LIVING OUT OTHER PEOPLE'S DREAMS. YOU HAVE YOUR OWN PATH TO TAKE AND YOU'LL FIND SUCCESS IN YOUR OWN WAYS."

—TRACY CHOU

TRACY CHOU

POP ART

Pop art uses popular images to create new art. Make your own pop art creation.

1. Choose a video from the Backgrounds tab. From the Graphics tab, click an image. You will repeat this graphic for your pop art creation.

2. Use a loop to tell the computer to repeat lines of code. Select the for block from the Effects tab.

3. Let's repeat this graphic five times. Your code should say:

```
4  var my_graphic1 = graphic("astronaut.png");
5
6  for (var i = 0; i < 5; i++) {
7      // Your code here
8  }
```

4. Set properties for the graphic before the for loop by coding the variables for each property.

```
3 var graphicX = 0;
4 var graphicY = 0;
5 var opacityAmount = 1;
6 var graphicScale = 0.7;
7 for (var i = 0; i < 5; i++) {
```

5. Inside the for loop, set the properties of the graphic.

```
1 movie = video();
2 movie.source = "night-stars.mp4";
3 var graphicX = 0;
4 var graphicY = 0;
5 var opacityAmount = 1;
6 var graphicScale = 0.7;
7 for (var i = 0; i < 5; i++) {
8       // Your code here
9 }
10 var my_graphic1 = graphic("astronaut.png");
```

6. The images are stacked on top of one another. To see them all, change their position and opacity.

7. See what else you can change!

```
1 movie = video();
2 movie.source = "night-stars.mp4";
3 var graphicX = 0;
4 var graphicY = 0;
5 var opacityAmount = 1;
6 var graphicScale = 0.7;
7 for (var i = 0; i < 5; i++) {
8       // Your code here
9
10    var my_graphic1 = graphic("astronaut.png")
11    my_graphic1.x = graphicX;
12    my_graphic1.y = graphicY;
13    my_graphic1.opacity = opacityAmount;
14    my_graphic1.scale = graphicScale;
15
16    graphicX += 120;
17    opacityAmount -= 0.2;
18 }    graphicScale -= 0.1;
```

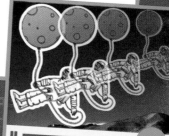

LYNDSEY SCOTT

1984–

TOP MODEL AND APP DEVELOPER

LYNDSEY SCOTT STARTED PROGRAMMING WHEN SHE WAS IN MIDDLE SCHOOL, creating fun games on her graphing calculator. She went on to learn coding skills in college while studying theater and computer science. After graduation, Scott worked as a top fashion model while also developing apps for mobile devices.

Scott is passionate about educating young women. She teaches girls to code through tutorials on her website, by mentoring for Girls Who Code, and by contributing to Code.org's Hour of Code. She joined Stack Overflow, the popular online community for coders, and answered questions on computer programming. Scott campaigns for women and people of color to have more opportunities to pursue STEM careers.

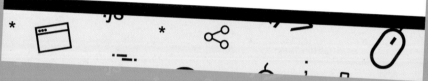

> "I THINK GIRLS IN GENERAL SHOULD JUST PUT THEIR FEAR ASIDE WHEN THEY GO TO THEIR CLASSES. IT'S IMPORTANT TO PARTICIPATE. IT'S IMPORTANT TO BE HEARD AND NOT LET THE STEREOTYPES STOP YOU."
>
> —LYNDSEY SCOTT

LYNDSEY SCOTT

CODE ON!

From the early days of computers, women have been super coders, fearless visionaries, and tech-savvy pioneers. And there is still so much to accomplish! You could be the next superstar to shake up the tech world. Are you ready?

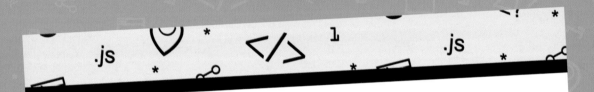

SOURCE NOTES

9   Ada Lovelace, in Miranda Seymour, *In Byron's Wake: The Turbulent Lives of Lord Byron's Wife and Daughter, Anabella Milbanke and Ada Lovelace* (New York: Pegasus, 2018), 227.

13   Grace Hopper, in Chris DiBona, Sam Ockman, and Mark Stone, *Open Sources: Voices from the Open Source Revolution* (Sebastopol, CA: O'Reilly, 1999), 7.

17   Annie Easley, "NASA Headquarters Oral History Project Edited Oral History Transcript," NASA, August 21, 2001, https://historycollection.jsc.nasa.gov/JSCHistoryPortal/history/oral_histories/NASA_HQ /Herstory/EasleyAJ/EasleyAJ_8-21-01.htm.

21   Margaret Hamilton, in Elizabeth Schmermund, *Telescopes, Probes, Spacecraft, and the Future of Space Exploration* (New York: Cavendish Square, 2017), 56.

25   Tracy Chou, in "15 Questions with Tracy Chou," CNN Business, accessed January 21, 2020, https://money .cnn.com/interactive/technology/15-questions-with-tracy-chou/index.html.

29   Lyndsey Scott, in "Lyndsey Scott: Runway Model and Tech Programmer," *Tell Me More*, NPR, March 20, 2014, https://www.npr.org/2014/03/20/291896460/lyndsey-scott-runway-model-and-tech-programmer.

GLOSSARY

ARRAY: a list of values

CONDITIONAL: lines in a code that tell a computer to do different things depending on if they are true or false, usually if-else statements

ENTREPRENEUR: one who organizes, manages, and takes on the risks of a business

GLITCH: to malfunction unexpectedly

HYBRID: having both a combustion engine and an electric motor

LOOP: in programming, a sequence of instructions that continually repeat until a condition is met

OBJECT: a container or an entity that can have properties and methods

OPACITY: how transparent an object is

PERSEVERANCE: the action of keeping at something in spite of difficulties, opposition, or discouragement

PROPERTY: value that belongs to an object

START-UP: a fledgling business

STEREOTYPE: an idea, often untrue, that many people have about a thing or group

VARIABLE: a container that can store a value

MORE ABOUT VIDCODE

Vidcode is a company founded by women whose mission is to encourage girls to enter the field of computer science. Vidcode's JavaScript-based platform lets users play with media such as images and videos to help learn to code and have fun doing it.

INDEX

PHOTO ACKNOWLEDGMENTS

Artwork by Margaret Sarah Carpenter courtesy of UK National Archives, p. 9; Bettmann/Getty Images, p. 13; NASA, p. 17; Clicker-Free-Vector-Images/Pixabay CC0, pp. 18–19 (rainbow); Charles Stark Draper Laboratory, Inc. via Smithsonian National Air and Space Museum (NASM2015-06488), p. 21; Michael Loccisano/Getty Images, p. 25; Stuart C. Wilson/Getty Images for TheirWorld, p. 29.

Cover and design elements: Big_and_serious/Getty Images (coding girl); zaieiu/Getty Images; yourbordo/Getty Images. Screenshots of projects by Sheela Preuitt.

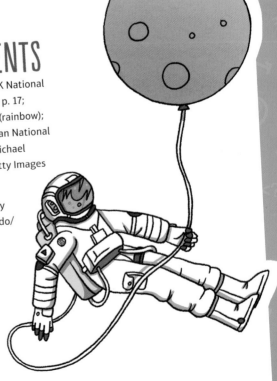

Pine River Library
395 Bayfield Center Dr.
P.O. Box 227
Bayfield, CO 81122
(970) 884-2222
www.prlibrary.org